If you have a home computer with Internet access you may:
- request an item to be placed on hold.
- renew an item that is not overdue or on hold.
- view titles and due dates checked out on your card.
- view and/or pay your outstanding fines online (over $5).

To view your patron record from your home computer click on Patchogue-Medford Library's homepage: www.pmlib.org

MARINE CORPS

Civilian to MARINE

by Meish Goldish

Consultant: Fred Pushies
U.S. SOF Adviser

BEARPORT
PUBLISHING

New York, New York

Credits

Cover and Title Page, © U.S. Marine Corps/Lance Cpl. David Castillo and U.S. Marine Corps/Lance Cpl. Caleb Gomez; 4, © 2007, Rick Loomis/Reprinted with permission of Los Angeles Times; 5, © 2007, Rick Loomis/Reprinted with permission of Los Angeles Times; 6, © Zuma Press/Newscom; 7T, © Scott Olson/Getty Images; 7B, © Scott Olson/Getty Images; 8, © U.S. Marine Corps/Cpl. Erik S. Anderson; 9L, © U.S. Marine Corps/Staff Sgt. Ken Tinnin; 9R, © Scott Olson/Getty Images; 10L, © U.S. Marine Corps/Sgt Cory A. Tepfenhart; 10R, © U.S. Marine Corps; 11, © Shannon Stapleton/Reuters/Landov; 12, © U.S. Marine Corps/Cpl. Justin J. Shemanski; 13, © 2007, Rick Loomis/Reprinted with permission of Los Angeles Times; 14, © Zuma Press/Newscom; 15T, © Zuma Press/Newscom; 15B, © U.S. Marine Corps; 16, © Jahi Chikwendiu/The Washington Post/Getty Images; 17, © Joe McNally/Getty Images; 18, © U.S. Marine Corps/Lance Cpl. Vernon T. Meekins; 19T, © Stephen Morton/Getty Images; 19B, © U.S. Marine Corps/Cpl. Shawn Dickens; 20, © Newscom; 21, © U.S. Marine Corps/Lance Cpl. James Clark; 22, © Scott Olson/Getty Images.

Publisher: Kenn Goin
Senior Editor: Lisa Wiseman
Creative Director: Spencer Brinker
Design: Debrah Kaiser
Photo Researcher: Picture Perfect Professionals, LLC

Library of Congress Cataloging-in-Publication Data

Goldish, Meish.
  Marine Corps : civilian to marine / by Meish Goldish; consultant, Fred Pushies.
    p. cm. — (Becoming a soldier)
  Includes bibliographical references and index.
  ISBN-13: 978-1-936088-13-3 (library binding)
  ISBN-10: 1-936088-13-4 (library binding)
  1. United States. Marine Corps—Juvenile literature. I. Pushies, Fred J., 1952– II. Title.
  VE23.G65 2011
  359.9'6540973—dc22
                              2010013665

For more information, write to Bearport Publishing Company, Inc., 101 Fifth Avenue, Suite 6R, New York, New York 10003. Printed in the United States of America in North Mankato, Minnesota.

072010
042110CGD

10 9 8 7 6 5 4 3 2 1

Contents

The Death March

A line of **recruits** dressed in full **combat** gear hiked steadily up the mountain. Their backs ached under the heavy weight of their 65-pound (29-kg) packs. Their feet were sore and burned with blisters. Some recruits limped in pain. Yet the sweaty recruits couldn't stop to rest. This 10-mile (16-km) march was a test. Were they tough enough to become part of the U.S. Marine Corps?

Marine recruits call this 10-mile (16-km) hike "the death march" because it is so hard to complete.

One recruit in the group, Steven Dellinger, welcomed the challenge. "I love how the Marines train really hard-core," he said. "I like their pride, the way they make you work so hard to accomplish stuff so that it really means something to you."

The Marine Corps is the part of the **armed forces** that carries out **military** operations on land as well as at sea.

Steven Dellinger went through many painful physical tests in order to become a Marine.

Welcome to Boot Camp

Steven had **enlisted** in the Marines in 2007, after graduating from high school. He reported to a recruit **depot** in San Diego, California, for basic training—also known as **boot camp**. This is a very intense 12-week program that all male and female recruits must pass to become Marines. They're taught battle skills and learn about Marine history and values.

These recruits have just arrived at the recruit depot in San Diego. Marine boot camp is longer than basic training for any other branch of the armed forces, including the army.

Marine basic training is held at only two recruit depots. The one in San Diego, California, is for all men who live west of the Mississippi River. The depot at Parris Island, South Carolina, is for all men east of the Mississippi. All female recruits are trained at Parris Island.

● U.S. Marine Recruit Basic Training Depots

After arriving at boot camp, recruits first receive their uniforms and get their hair cut. Their new look reminds them that they are no longer **civilians**. Now they're in the military.

Male recruits get their heads shaved, while female recruits just have to get short haircuts.

Recruits wearing their new uniforms and holding their packs with new gear wait for their next order.

The Drill Instructor

Wearing their new uniforms and sporting short haircuts, the recruits are placed into 80-member groups called **platoons**. Men and women are grouped separately. Three or four **drill instructors** are in charge of each platoon for the rest of basic training.

A drill instructor and his platoon

Drill instructors are often loud, angry-sounding, and very strict. Their most important job is to teach the platoon to follow orders. To do this, they shout directly into the face of any recruit who makes a mistake. For example, someone whose shoes are not shined will be yelled at and told to do push-ups or sit-ups as a punishment. The punishment helps the recruit remember not to make the same mistake twice!

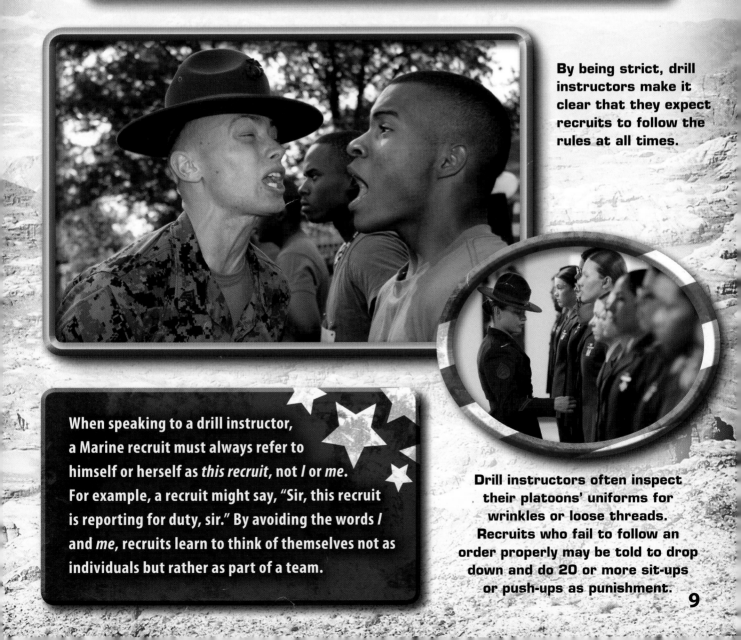

By being strict, drill instructors make it clear that they expect recruits to follow the rules at all times.

When speaking to a drill instructor, a Marine recruit must always refer to himself or herself as *this recruit*, not *I* or *me*. For example, a recruit might say, "Sir, this recruit is reporting for duty, sir." By avoiding the words *I* and *me*, recruits learn to think of themselves not as individuals but rather as part of a team.

Drill instructors often inspect their platoons' uniforms for wrinkles or loose threads. Recruits who fail to follow an order properly may be told to drop down and do 20 or more sit-ups or push-ups as punishment.

Physical Training

Drill instructors know that Marines must be strong to succeed in battle. So physical training is a very important part of boot camp. By 6:30 each morning, the recruits have already begun their training. They start with set after set of knee bends, leg lifts, toe touches, and arm twirls. Those are followed by dozens of push-ups, sit-ups, and pull-ups. With aching muscles, the recruits are then required to run two to four miles (3.2 to 6.4 km). Though they're exhausted, the recruits know they must finish the run.

Recruits during a run

In order to become Marines, recruits must pass a tough physical fitness test. Male recruits must complete at least 3 pull-ups, 50 **crunches** in 2 minutes, and a 3 mile run (4.8 km) in 28 minutes. Female recruits must be able to do at least a 15-second **flexed arm hang**, 50 crunches in 2 minutes, and a 3 mile (4.8 km) run in 31 minutes.

A Marine doing the flexed arm hang

Drill instructors push their platoons harder and harder each day. When a tired recruit thinks he or she can do no more, it is called "hitting the wall." Instructors give **pep talks** to encourage the recruit to keep going and train even harder.

Drill instructors help recruits learn to push themselves to their physical limits and beyond.

Gaining Confidence

To push themselves further, recruits must feel confident in their physical abilities. They build their self-confidence by training on a **Confidence Course**. This is a series of 11 **treacherous obstacles** that each recruit must master. On one of the more demanding obstacles, the Confidence Climb, recruits must climb up, over, and down a giant ladder-like object made of logs that rises 30 feet (9.1 m) into the air. That's like climbing a three-story building!

The Confidence Course helps increase the recruits' physical strength as well as their confidence.

An even more terrifying obstacle is the Slide for Life. Recruits must make their way along a long **cable** that stretches over a swimming pool. Many recruits lose their grip and fall into the water on their first try.

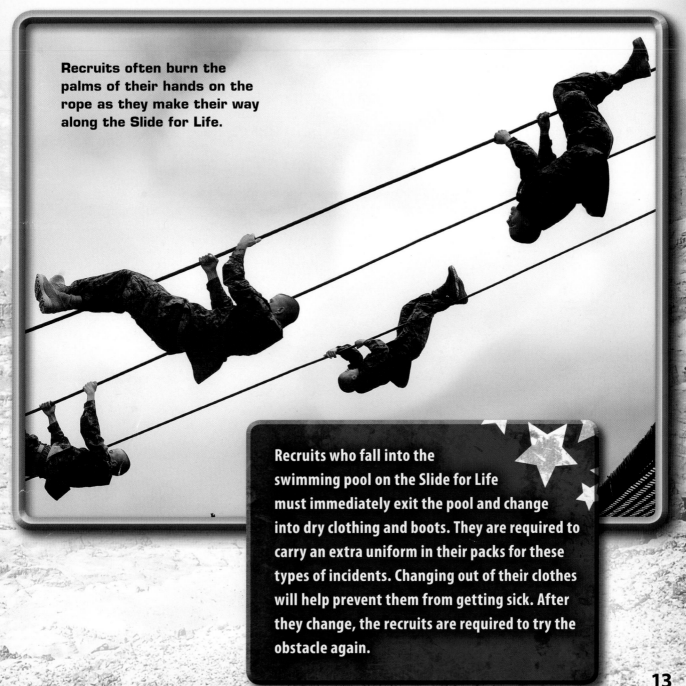

Recruits often burn the palms of their hands on the rope as they make their way along the Slide for Life.

Recruits who fall into the swimming pool on the Slide for Life must immediately exit the pool and change into dry clothing and boots. They are required to carry an extra uniform in their packs for these types of incidents. Changing out of their clothes will help prevent them from getting sick. After they change, the recruits are required to try the obstacle again.

A Recruit's Best Friend

During boot camp, recruits learn how to use many weapons, including knives. However, it's the M16 rifle that is a Marine's best protection in combat. Recruits are taught how to **assemble** and shoot their weapons. They spend long hours practicing their aim and firing their rifles. Learning how to accurately shoot their rifles gives them the confidence they need to protect themselves and others during battle.

Recruits spend long hours on the rifle range.

Recruits also learn to take apart their rifles and clean them. A clean weapon is less likely to jam or misfire in battle. After weeks of practice, recruits are so used to taking the M16 apart and then cleaning and reassembling it that they can do it with their eyes closed.

Recruits practice using their rifles in a combat exercise.

During basic training, recruits are required to memorize the Rifleman's **Creed**. The words of the creed remind recruits of just how important their rifles are to their survival.

Female recruits practicing taking apart their rifles

A Gas Attack

Sometimes rifles alone aren't enough to protect Marines. They need to be prepared for anything, even a deadly gas attack. During boot camp, recruits are taught how to survive such an attack by wearing a gas mask.

Recruits wearing their gas masks

After learning to breathe with their gas masks on, the recruits spend three to five minutes in a **chamber** filled with tear gas. These few minutes can feel endless to the nervous recruits. Once inside, they are told to remove their masks and breathe in a little bit of the gas. Instantly, it makes their eyes tear up and their skin burn. Gas in their lungs makes them cough. At this point, recruits usually start to panic because they feel as if they've lost control. Finally, they're allowed to put their masks back on and leave the chamber.

The gas chamber, shown here, contains gas that cannot kill but can make recruits feel sick.

Recruits are forced to breathe the tear gas with and without their masks to help them gain confidence in using their masks. They learn by experience that the mask keeps the gas from harming them.

The Final Test

After about three months of training, recruits face their final and most difficult test—the Crucible. During a 54-hour period, they work in teams to complete a number of physical tasks that will push their **endurance** to the limit. For example, in one challenge they have to climb up a three-story structure with all their heavy gear, and rescue a person trapped on the roof. Teammates help one another as they use every bit of strength to make their way up and down.

Here, the recruits work together to rescue a person on the roof of a tall structure.

Other challenges include **simulated** war attacks and rescues of fellow platoon members who are injured in battle. The Crucible ends with a painful nine-to-ten-mile (14.4-to-16-km) march in the middle of the night. During the Crucible, recruits get very little to eat and only about three hours of sleep each night—just like the conditions they might face in a real war.

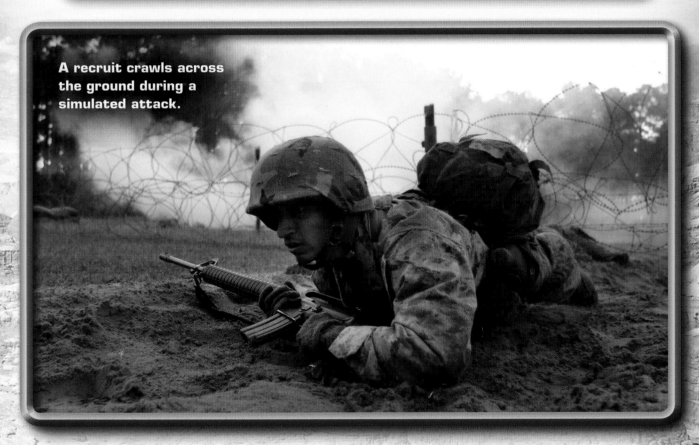

A recruit crawls across the ground during a simulated attack.

Recruits celebrate their completion of the Crucible with a Warriors' Breakfast. This huge meal consists of eggs, steak, bacon, pancakes, and waffles.

After completing the Crucible, recruits receive the Marine Corps Emblem—the Eagle, Globe, and Anchor badge. This means that they are now officially Marines.

Moving On

At boot camp graduation, platoons march together to show how they work as a team. After a ten-day break, the Marines then move on to advanced training. Some, such as Steven Dellinger, train as **infantry** fighters. After his advanced training, Steven went on to fight **overseas** in Iraq.

A platoon salutes during graduation.

Other Marines train for jobs that support the infantry. For example, some become **mechanics** who fix trucks and tanks. No matter how they serve, all Marines proudly dedicate themselves to the Marine Corps values—honor, courage, and commitment. They live up to their motto: "Always faithful."

Marines at work in Afghanistan

Recruits in the Marines usually enlist for four to six years. A person can also choose to make the Marines a lifetime career.

Preparing for the Marine Corps

If you are interested in joining the U.S. Marines in the future, you can start preparing now by doing well in school, keeping your body in top physical shape, and being a responsible person. According to the U.S. government, the following rules also apply:

★ You must be between 18 and 29 years old. You can enlist at the age of 17 but need your parents' written permission.

★ You should have a high school diploma.

★ You cannot have a serious criminal record.

★ Males must be no shorter than 5′ 5″ inches (1.65 m) and no taller than 6′ 5″ inches (1.96 m). Females must be no shorter than 4′ 8″ inches (1.42 m) and no taller than 6′ 0″ (1.83 m).

★ You must pass a Marine job skills test that measures your language, math, and science skills.

★ You may also need to pass a physical fitness test.

Glossary

armed forces (ARMD FORSS-iz) the military groups a country uses to protect itself; in the United States these are the Army, the Navy, the Air Force, the Marines, and the Coast Guard

assemble (uh-SEM-buhl) to put all the parts of something together

boot camp (BOOT KAMP) a place where Navy or Marine recruits go for basic training

cable (KAY-buhl) a thick wire or rope

chamber (CHAYM-bur) a closed-in room

civilians (si-VIL-yuhnz) people who are not members of the armed forces

combat (KOM-bat) having to do with fighting between people or armies

Confidence Course (KON-fuh-duhnss KORSS) a training course that is filled with obstacles such as walls to climb or bridges to cross that recruits must complete

creed (KREED) a statement of beliefs; words that one lives by

crunches (KRUHNCH-iz) exercises that require a person to lie on his or her back and then lift the upper body partway off the floor

depot (DEE-poh) a place where recruits or new soldiers gather

drill instructors (DRIL in-STRUHK-turz) people who are in charge of a group of recruits during basic training

endurance (en-DUR-uhnss) the ability or strength to continue despite bad conditions

enlisted (en-LIST-id) joined a branch of the armed forces

flexed arm hang (FLEKST ARM HANG) a type of exercise where a person grasps an overhead bar as if he or she is doing a pull-up; the person must keep his or her chin above the bar and hold the position for as long as possible

infantry (IN-fuhn-tree) the part of an army that fights on foot

mechanics (muh-KAN-iks) people who are skilled at fixing machines

military (MIL-uh-*ter*-ee) the armed forces of a country

obstacles (OB-stuh-kuhlz) objects in a person's path such as fences or walls that he or she must be able to get over

overseas (oh-vur-SEEZ) across the ocean

pep talks (PEP TAWKS) short speeches given to a person or group of people in order to inspire or encourage

platoons (pluh-TOONZ) groups of recruits who live and train together

recruits (ri-KROOTS) people who have recently joined the armed forces

simulated (SIM-yuh-*lay*-tid) pretended to be like something real

treacherous (TRECH-ur-uhss) very dangerous

Index

Bibliography

Keeter, Hunter. *The U.S. Marine Corps.* Milwaukee, WI: World Almanac (2005).

Stein, R. Conrad. *The U.S. Marine Corps and Military Careers.* Berkeley Heights, NJ: Enslow (2006).

Read More

Benson, Michael. *The U.S. Marine Corps.* Minneapolis, MN: Lerner (2005).

Sandler, Michael. *Marine Force Recon in Action.* New York: Bearport Publishing (2008).

Learn More Online

To learn more about the U.S. Marine Corps, visit
www.bearportpublishing.com/BecomingaSoldier

About the Author

Meish Goldish has written more than 200 books for children. He lives in Brooklyn, New York.